# Tara Bernerd · Place

# Tara Bernerd

TEXTS BY CHARLOTTE & PETER FIELL

# Place

# Contents

Portrait by Graciela Cattarossi

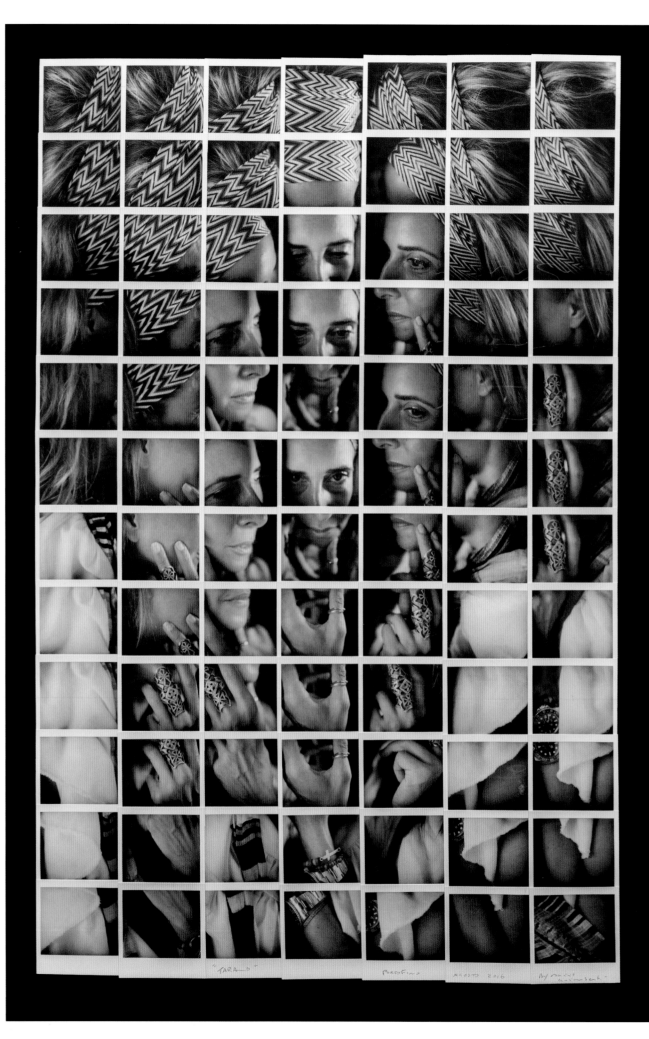

# Preface

So far mine has been an extraordinary journey of learning about people and places. Ultimately my work has been about trying to comprehend what people desire from a space whilst respecting the place itself and honoring the indigenous character of each project.

My projects have been about not only my invaluable clients, who invariably become great friends, but also my incredible team, who have worked diligently, evolved, and matured. I think the value of the care we feel has brought us to a place where we can now share some of our stories.

From the moment I started, there was, and indeed still is, a great sense of responsibility that comes with the privilege of being asked to create something. Anticipating and then visualizing a home, a space, a hotel is all about aiming to achieve through design an atmosphere that will somehow lift one's experience.

For me, every project has its own demands that determine how it should be approached. Beginning with the interior architecture of a space, our intelligent layouts and space-planning are the foundation of our work, allowing us to consider the lifestyle of a place and ensuring we can provide an environment that will have just the right effect on its users.

The world today moves at an exceptional pace; however, trends are something I have avoided—and perhaps rules, too. For me, the most important aspect of design is seeking the components that are authentic, that will stand true in time.

And yet design is also way beyond the final look. As in the film industry, behind the scenes is where the real work, and indeed the talent, exists; it is where the hidden "secrets" of our industry labor tirelessly to ensure that our creations can be born and ultimately shared.

This book is dedicated to my partners and our far-reaching, brilliant teams. Our sense of loyalty and beliefs are the constant drivers, as are the friendships formed over decades together.

I am increasingly asked that rather awkward question, "What do you want out of life?" My answer is simple: to keep moving forward.

Tara Bernerd

Portrait by Maurizio Galimberti © Instant Artist

# Foreword

It has been a pleasure to follow Tara's work over the
past fifteen years. She has managed to develop a very
personal and beautiful design language. Her work has
a strong sense of space and by skilfully incorporating
beautiful materials she is able to imbue her schemes
with a feeling of comfort that is both personal and
modern. Whatever space she designs is particular to
its use; wood, stone, plaster, carpet, textiles all combine
to give it a rare sensuality.

Richard Rogers

Portrait by Benedict Johnson

# Working with Tara

I originally met Tara as a teenager while traveling for the first time in the South of France. It was quite an eye opener for a teenager from the suburbs of New York City. I made some amazing friendships over that summer and we collectively enjoyed a vibrant, adventurous time that can only be experienced through the eyes of youth and the spirit of unlimited potential.

Over the years, Tara and I more or less lost touch, living on different continents and pursuing our own interests, formulating what would be our professional selves. In 2007, however, a mutual friend from that special summer suggested we get back in touch. Tara was now working in interior design, and at that time my brothers and I had decided to take our growing Thompson boutique hotel chain over to Europe.

Our team identified a wonderful site in Belgravia, London—a stone's throw from Tara's office. We arranged a meeting and instantly reconnected on a creative level. In many ways, Tara and I were at similar stages in our emerging careers, and we shared many of the same ideas about the reinterpretation of luxury. She was able to intuitively capture and visually express what I was thinking on that first project together—Belgraves.

We have since collaborated on other hotels and Tara has repeatedly shown an innate sense of how to make a site take life and speak to the audience we're targeting. When it came time to move on and create a new brand—SIXTY—we immediately turned to Tara to work with us through the birthing process. The first result was SIXTY SoHo, which ideally captures the eclectic, casual sophistication that is the foundation of our aesthetic spirit.

When working on a project we often visualize an ideal guest, a figure that embodies the brand sensibilities and creative spirit we're designing for. Tara in many ways embodies that profile; her global wanderlust and unique personal style are what our brand is all about. She is constantly traveling and, more important, seeking out those small inspirations that are the seedlings for so many great ideas—ideas that are culturally savvy, forward-thinking, but never contrived.

She has helped define the phrase "rough luxury" and proven herself a virtual magician in figuring out and reshaping spaces. I believe our collaborations have taken a cinematic approach. Unlike some designers who look at a project's overall space and try to divide it into smaller pieces, Tara instead focuses on one area and then visually pans out, like a film director.

She is also able to sensitively and quickly grasp the individual DNA of a project, which for me is essential because my hotels are neighborhood-centric and need that level of personalization to work. Perhaps most important, Tara is emotionally vested in all her projects. She genuinely cares and stays connected and passionate about her work and her clients long after the design brief has been completed.

I am truly proud of our collaborations. That being said, I know our best work is still to come.

Jason Pomeranc

Portrait by Randall Slavin

Chalet Miramonti, Gstaad:
Hallway with artwork by Tracey Emin

# Introduction

# A Sense of Place

Tara Bernerd has earned a reputation as one of today's foremost interior architectural designers. An avowed design crusader who believes that design can and should make a difference, Tara lives and breathes the projects she undertakes with her close-knit team of architects and designers. Having cut her creative teeth in Philippe Starck's YOO design studio during the 1990s, she went on to found her own interior architecture practice in London in 2002. Since then she has become renowned as much for her handsome signature style as for her genius with interior space planning. Straddling the worlds of residential, hospitality, and commercial property development, Tara has created a plethora of beautiful and innovative interiors across the globe that have attracted widespread critical acclaim, from elegant private homes, über-stylish super yachts, and dramatic office headquarters to luxurious hotels, sexy and seductive nightclubs, and chic yet classic restaurants. She has even designed a ski chalet, a hunting lodge, and a number of treehouses. The thread running through all these projects is Tara's approach to problem solving, which is both human-centric and design-intelligent. It is the reason her interiors look and work the way they do. Many of these are featured on the pages of this book and are notable for their engaging sense of warmth and character. Tara's work represents a new and more culturally savvy direction in interior design: one that acknowledges in an increasingly globalized, atomized world, in which people travel far more than ever before, that we all want to feel at home regardless of where we are. Whether in our private residences, or a hotel lobby, or even a restaurant, we all seek meaning and connection through a sense of place.

# Albion Riverside Apartment

LATITUDE: 51.4, LONGITUDE: -0.1

LOCATION: BATTERSEA, LONDON, UK

CLIENT: SELF

COMPLETED: 2013

As a case study, Tara Bernerd's own residence in the Battersea district of London works well in that it completely embodies her design philosophy. As she explains, "I maximized the open-plan living area by reducing the number of bedrooms and introduced some great materials, from concrete and steel to petrol-blue leather and travertine." Located within a landmark Foster + Partners building, the flat has incredible views not just of the River Thames but also of buildings on the other side of the Embankment.

"When I first walked in," Bernerd says, "my approach was to look at this space in terms of lifestyle. So in many ways it was no different from any other project, because I invariably look at each case from a personal perspective, as if it was me living in it." One aspect that initially attracted her to the apartment was its proximity to the river. Essentially starting with a blank canvas, Bernerd and her team undertook a careful space-planning evaluation with the knowledge that because the apartment was located in an existing building, the ability to move many walls was limited. The outcome was the decision to change the configuration from three en-suite bedrooms to two, plus a study and a guest cloakroom. Bernerd effectively cannibalized the original third bathroom and "cut into it from all sides" to create a bigger master bathroom with more closet space while leaving room for a small guest washroom. A solid wall between the lobby and living area was also knocked through, replaced by iron-framed glazed Crittall doors to create an industrial-chic quality while also framing a stunning vista of the river from the entranceway. In addition, the lobby was transformed into a gallery-like space by using smooth cast-concrete panels and a large reflecting mirror. This moody room, in which a small Keith McCarter bronze is spot-lit to perfection, leads into the open-plan living area, where a relatively neutral palette is offset by the colorful impact of large artworks and an array of thoughtfully chosen and strategically placed objects. Throughout the 2,000-square-foot apartment, Bernerd and her team's unique interior style plays out at its very best through a striking contrast of rough materials set against luxurious ones, as well as by an interesting and eclectic mix of meaningful art and decorative objects. The open-plan living area is cleverly divided by a bespoke bookcase-cum-fireplace that separates the main living space from a more intimate, cocooned seating area. But perhaps the most eye-catching element is a pair of enormous photographic portraits of carrier pigeons taken by the artist Geoff Weston.

The overall impression is of luxurious modern comfort with an edge, which is what Bernerd is renowned for. Eclectically mixing contemporary pieces with midcentury modern collectibles, she displays a thorough understanding of the rich visual rhythms that one can achieve by incorporating both new and vintage. Her collection of design classics in the living area reveals a savvy eye at work, as evidenced by the Stilnovo floor lamp, Louis Kalff table light, pair of Sergio Rodrigues armchairs, and set of PK9 dining chairs by Poul Kjaerholm. Bernerd also understands the dramatic power of large-scale art to pull together an interior scheme and give it a special identity all its own. Here she has incorporated, among other artworks, a large canvas by Harland Miller entitled *A Decisive Blow Against If*, which Bernerd especially likes because, as she notes, "I'm someone who chooses not to live my life by saying 'What if?'" But it is the smaller details that give an almost jewel-like quality to the apartment—from smoky Murano ashtrays to a wonderful collection of old books dating from the 1950s through the 1970s. Above all, this home epitomizes Tara Bernerd's uniquely handsome style of interior architecture, the result of being carefully built up layer by layer, from layout and spec to finishes, furnishings, and details.

Artwork by Harland Miller: *A Decisive Blow Against If*, 2012

Lobby area with rough-cut concrete walls and
mirrored glass doors. Artwork by Erwin Olaf.

Sculpture by Keith McCarter.
Artwork from Terry O'Neill's 'Icons' series.

Pair of 'Kilin' armchairs by Sergio Rodrigues. Tarantula
artwork from Guido Mocafico's 'Aranea' series. Carrier
pigeon artwork from Geoff Weston's 'Messengers' series.

Balcony overlooking Albert Bridge and
the River Thames

Master suite with artwork (left) by Jack Pierson,
courtesy Cheim & Read, New York and artwork (right)
by James Nares, courtesy Paul Kasmin, New York

Petrol blue leather panelled wall.
Artwork by Terry O'Neill.

# Past

CF: *I know that you are more interested in the present and the future than in the past. But we should probably start at the beginning. You must have been interested in design when you were growing up. When did you first become consciously aware of design?*

TB: What fascinates me is not necessarily how I've grown as a designer, but how people's lifestyles have changed and how the world is evolving at such an incredible rate. As a child, I had vinyl records and no iPhone—in fact no mobile at all—and because of that we communicated differently, we even spoke differently. Likewise, the concept of the family has changed, too, and it is all those aspects of life that have an impact on how we live. So what I find interesting about looking back is seeing how design has been affected. And asking in what way design may demand to be different tomorrow.

I'm very interested in how some areas of design evolve, but others never change; for instance, the sanctuary and coziness of a bedroom is still something that, despite all the technology in the world, we hold sacred. However, there are other living areas, where we eat, drink, or communicate, that are certainly influenced by today's new lifestyles. And projecting forward, it is fascinating to contemplate what the future will be like and how people are going to live.

*Do you think the increased knowledge about design has changed people's design expectations?*

Certainly, design has become integral to our understanding of lifestyle. But it is naïve to think that we are living in the "design decade" just because we have a more design-savvy audience. You can go back to the '30s, the midcentury era, the '60s and '70s, etc., and see how strong interior design always was. If you go back even further, to the eighteenth and nineteenth centuries, you can find extraordinary examples of design excellence. In fact, if one dives into the history of design, the list is endless. For instance, Pierre Chareau's Maison de Verre in Paris, built in the late 1920s/early 1930s, was an outstanding example of innovative interior design. So I don't think that having creative design juice in us is something unique to our times, but the greater accessibility to excellent design most definitely is.

*Looking back, what do you think were the key drivers behind this democratization of design?*

The past and how it relates to my own work is in many ways connected to the explosion of design-led television shows and magazines in the late '80s and early '90s. All of a sudden the newspaper supplements had become design savvy, resulting in an increasing need for ever more design-specific editorial pages. The media suddenly realized that design sells. As a result, it started to be a tangible business proposition, for design was no longer seen as an affectation of the rich but was fast becoming a significant part of everybody's lifestyles. It was above all aspirational, with the vibe being that everybody deserves to find a way to make their homes as good looking and functionally efficient as they could be.

*It was indeed extraordinary how design began to infiltrate the mainstream. What were the aspects of that exciting period that stand out most in your memory?*

I think it was the idea that everybody could take an interest in the design of their homes, and this concept ensured that TV shows blossomed. It was that, more than anything else, that was the beginning of a definable shift whereby interior design, which had perhaps been previously seen as elitist, was now viewed as something for everyone. I was definitely part of that crusade, which saw design morphing into a serious business activity, or at least a key consideration when creating one's home. Personally, I was blessed in that I spent some time working in the studios of YOO with Philippe Starck. Looking back I see myself as being part of a band of design-passionate people, and for me that era will always remain "the design crusade years." We were putting

Portrait © Bob Carlos Clarke

out there that design did matter. At YOO we changed the prevailing "location, location, location" mindset and effectively said "no," it can instead be "location, location, design."

*Your first interior design project was a loft space in Battersea, and it really helped kick off your career. What was it like?*

It was one of my earlier projects, and was only about 500 meters from my current apartment. It was in an old riverside tobacco factory right by Ransome's Dock, above what was then Café Rouge. At this point Battersea was not perceived as a great location.

Although it was one of my first notable projects, it was very true to the design DNA that still exists in me today. Appointing and working with architect Pankaj Patel on the project was also a cherished learning experience. It was all about space; it was about leaving space, filling space, and it was about raw materials, wood and concrete.

*Was it also about being true to the industrial heritage of the building, or at least channeling it?*

I think the concept for a project usually comes from an authentic response to the space—what city is it in, what's the climate like, what type of building is it? The reason for flagging this example was, yes, the finishes and perhaps how it looked were inspired by the existing structure. But the most important thing was that it powerfully reinforced in me the belief that design mattered.

*Did you gain confidence by putting it together and seeing it work? If I remember correctly, you also won the Andrew Martin Interior Designer of the Year award for it. Surely that gave you the confidence to think, "I'm good at this and I'm going to run with it." Or did you know that already?*

For me, confidence is in continuously short supply. But I think seeing it work as a project did give me the courage to take another step. I do have a vast passion and enthusiasm for what I do, and every time we get a chance to do more, I just want to keep on doing more, and doing better. So I guess my confidence is growing.

*I know you have a real can-do spirit. Where do you think that came from?*

I have always had a can-do attitude. I'm not really sure why, but probably it's a mixture of energy and passion. I do have an abundance of energy, which is a necessary ingredient for what I

do. I think it runs in my family's blood. My father has legendary energy, which has helped him not only achieve extraordinary success in the financial and creative development worlds, but also to fight serious illness. Likewise, my mother is a force of nature. As a family, we also have a good sense of humor that helps when the going gets tough.

*You left school at sixteen and are ostensibly self-taught. How did that happen?*

I wanted to be independent. And being independent at an early age meant that I broke rules often without even realizing. While my parent's marital breakdown was undoubtedly challenging, it was also what formed me and encouraged me to break boundaries.

*After leaving school, you undertook a number of apprenticeships. How did these help in your later career?*

Everything I did fed what I do today. That's why I greatly value learning on the job. I also think growing up in a world where I didn't have that traditional family structure made me look elsewhere for role models. At the time, a powerful woman ran this country, and that gave me the belief that anything was possible. It wasn't just me who was affected. A lot of my girlfriends from that time have gone on to set incredible professional benchmarks.

*Certainly, it was the first generation of women who had grown up with the belief that you could do it all and have it all. I don't mean that we had a sense of entitlement, but rather that we were prepared to go all out for it in terms of having a career.*

I think we just grew up thinking it was okay to try. Fundamentally, my time working in commercial property helped shape what I do today. For several years I worked with an incredible group called Nelson Bakewell, and as the only girl trader on the floor I had to get my head around contracts, speaking to and meeting clients, and the ins and outs of financial purchases in property portfolios that were worth millions. I then became obsessed with the design of restaurants. Eventually I created a restaurant division for them, which is how I met the likes of Oliver Peyton and Julian Metcalfe. And whilst I eventually walked away from it to pursue a more creative career, I made sure I took with me every commercial and financial experience I had learned.

*Apart from having a handle on all the different aspects of running a project, from the creative to the financial, you must also be that type of level-headed person who is able to find a solution when things don't go according to plan.*

In many ways I'm putting out fires all day, but out of that comes some beautiful creative moments, when you go "Eureka!" and can see what that design should be. My father always says that what I do is like pushing elephants up a hill. As he puts it, "You're not a designer, you're a herds girl, and when you're pushing an elephant up a hill, you've got to make sure it doesn't slide and sit on your face." But sometimes you get to the top of the hill and you look around and you see what you've achieved, and that's a pretty amazing moment.

*Describing that "phew, we've done it" experience makes it sound a bit like mountaineering.*

Yes, but the only difference is that once you've finished the climb, the vista is one's own creation. Certainly, it is the exhilaration of the climb that keeps one going, and it's a relief to have a few minutes' respite from the elephant. But it doesn't last for long because there's always another elephant coming. We don't stand at the peak and admire the view for too long. Instead, we'll go to the left and set our sights on another peak.

*I remember you saying once that you were inspired by a children's program in which everything a boy drew turned into reality.*

I've always drawn, and when I was a child I drew endless characters. Even in my marriage I drew a lot, and my wonderful husband at the time, James Archer, used to have a gallery downstairs with all my pictures. And yes, I remember this cartoon when I was very young, which was called "Simon in the Land of Chalk Drawings." He was this little chalk boy and he would say, "My name is Simon and all the things I draw come true," and I remember being fascinated by this idea. When I look at a blank canvas, I see in my mind's eye the design I want to achieve, and then I sketch it. And through drawing I design a reality, just like Simon. When I stand back and look at people arriving for the opening party of a hotel we've designed, I never fail to remember the girl who watched that cartoon. It's a "One can make a picture come true!" kind of feeling, and that enthusiasm has never left me. Equally, my enthusiasm for travel, which has played a huge part in my career to date, has never left me either.

*So you're a bit of a design-fueled Duracell bunny that just keeps on going.*

It's the enthusiasm for my job that keeps me going. Often

I don't want to go on a trip because I don't want to leave anyone, but then once I get there it's "Snap! I'm here and I love it." I also have an ability to compartmentalize, which allows me to jump from one project to the next, and I never forget anything, even the smallest of details from project to project.

*Is that because you have a strong visual memory? Can you, for instance, recollect a certain layout configuration, a color tone, or a specific texture or material?*

I have an extraordinary visual memory, and I know right now every detail of every project we're working on. But then again, I'm terrible with dates.

*Do you believe that one can spiritually lift people with a well-designed space?*

Of course. The church was the first to cotton on to this fact with its building of the great cathedrals. With their sheer scale and the dazzling colors of their soaring stained-glass windows. It was in many ways intimidation by design, but it also took people into the spiritual realm.

I believe that providing well-designed environments does make people feel better, especially if the spaces have the quality of home. And that's a key word for me. What is home? Given that so many people are in transit nowadays, can a hotel ever take the place of home? And if so, how? When I started out on my design journey, you had hotels that were the iconic city landmarks—you had the Peninsula Hotel with its fleet of green Rolls Royces over in Hong Kong, and places like the Carlyle in New York, and then over here in London we had Claridge's or the Savoy. At that stage, boutique hotels had only just started to appear.

*It was Philippe Starck's Royalton Hotel in New York, which opened in 1988, that was the real breakthrough. It was an extraordinary stage set where people lived their lives as though in a goldfish bowl.*

At that time, Philippe Starck was one of the bigger names in design and he certainly played a role in the explosion of the so-called boutique hotel, which really means a smaller design-led place to stay.

*How did the big hotel groups respond to the challenge of the boutiques?*

Hotels are businesses, but it's not only a numbers game; they also have to understand people's needs and move with the times. The rise of the boutique hotel meant that the larger brands were having to adapt and evolve to stay relevant, because what the boutiques were offering was perhaps a more genuine experience and authentic feel, with a detailed attention to the different layers of design. They were creating some real gems and it began to alter what people were coming to demand from some of the bigger players. The big hotels have to, and indeed want to, face this challenge. Brands like Rosewood and Four Seasons began reinventing themselves to compete with what the smaller boutiques had to offer, and whilst they might not necessarily have had the youth of the boutique upstarts, they began creating that same feeling of authenticity, of a home away from home, on a larger scale. They understood that a brand name is not enough; what counts is the DNA of that brand. What are your philosophies? What are your core values? Once you are able to establish that and know who you are, then it becomes about delivering this message consistently and holistically within everything you do, from service and operations to design intent, across the entire guest experience.

*What I could never understand was why, in the 1990s and early 2000s, people would go to these designer hotels and then want to replicate the look in their own houses.*

But they absolutely did, because hotels impacted people's design sense, and they still do. I think it was a guidance they warmed to; even today, everyone wants to know what's the latest style, what's the current trend. Personally, I avoid trends. And I think my resistance to them comes from the fact that a lot of our past work can be seen as timeless. But people always want to be inspired, and it is understandable that we go to hotels and see something, and then we want a bit of that feeling in our own homes. I admire the interiors of such designers as David Collins because he never fell into being formulaic and he took a bit from different themes and ideas and made his own magical brew.

*Apart from learning from other designers, what did you gain while working with YOO that you were able to take with you on your journey?*

Philippe was a total design crusader, and he was as much an inspiration to me as John Hitchcox, who had created Manhattan Lofts and brought lofts to London, which was in itself a "wow" in design. Suddenly, we had brick walls and cool buildings and open plan. Their company, YOO, was really a marriage of their two minds, and while working with them both, I was absorbing everything. I learned lifestyle planning and interior architecture, and then there was Philippe's confidence of putting together a palette. From him I also learned that you mustn't dither, that you have to be decisive in your design decisions. Even to this

day, I'm involved in every project we're working on. Sometimes even if a plan—that has been presented but not signed—isn't working, I'm not ruthless or unkind, but I do say, "No, we have to start again, take that out and that out." And then I can see quite quickly what the solutions are.

*Really that's just a sign of a highly attuned eye.*

Yes, it is. It's just like being a good chef. The reason is that, for each project, I like to establish its DNA or flavor, and each one is different by its inherent nature and location. I'm not one of those interior designers who wants to have a replicated imprint of their style everywhere.

*That's what I think is so incredible about your work: you have a definable signature look, but at the same time you still manage to interpret different cultural contexts within it. What comes across in your work is a cultural savviness that is undoubtedly derived from your outward-looking perspective and love of traveling.*

I constantly absorb and observe when I'm traveling. I spent a lot of time as a kid in Asia, in Hong Kong and China. Since then my work has been my passport. But what I would say is that you can't rest on your laurels in this industry. Whatever work you do, it's the input that counts.

*I read somewhere that your mother had a credo that input equals output.*

Yes, she always said, "Input, output." I was brought up to never expect anything, and as a result, I feel the world owes me nothing. I'm lucky to have a place in it. I was brought up to think that you had to make an effort and give something.

*Meaning, having to make it happen and never relying on anything?*

Well, if you're not "can do," then what are you doing? When I was about eighteen, I wrote this proverb and I've always kept it. It goes: "One can hope, but not expect, and if one's hopes are built on expectations, there is no hope." I still believe this. We're lucky now because the hard work over the years has paid off, but of course we still need jobs coming in. We need to win the work. Hopefully the more we put out great product, the more jobs we'll be offered. And then we can choose the ones we really want to do. So in effect everything we do is building on the past, but we're also aware that you're only ever as good as your last project, so we have to put in 110 percent.

*Looking back, what stands out vis-à-vis how you got to the place in which you now find yourself as a designer?*

Without a shadow of a doubt it's the people. Indeed, without wishing to prioritize, I will always be indebted to those first clients who gave me the chance that has led me here. Tony Pidgley, chairman of the Berkeley Group, is one of those people and has formed a huge part of my career and confidence. He is a visionary and has been my rock throughout our countless projects together. Likewise, Jay Jopling also took a chance with me and we worked together early in my career, designing interiors for his White Cube galleries. There is an invaluable cast of clients, and indeed teammates, and they all mean so much.

# Chalet Miramonti

LATITUDE: 46.4, LONGITUDE: 7.2

LOCATION: GSTAAD, SWITZERLAND

CLIENT: PRIVATE

COMPLETED: 2008

This traditional chalet overlooks the Gstaad Valley in Switzerland and, as its name suggests, provides spectacular mountain views from both its windows and its terraces. Between 2007 and 2008, Chalet Miramonti was redesigned by Tara Bernerd & Partners. When undertaking the project, her team was mindful to retain the very Swiss sense of place; indeed, the building's traditional *Gemütlichkeit*, or relaxed coziness, is what makes it so special. The existing exterior was left more or less as it was, but a large, sympathetic extension was added, creating an entirely new wing. Similarly, the interiors were extended and remodeled extensively, with three subterranean levels excavated below the existing structure.

During the process, certain Helvetian references were knowingly and liberally quoted, yet in a completely contemporary way, such as the pine paneling used throughout the ground floor, the trunklike handrails of the new glass-sided staircase, and the local gray quartzite of the fireplaces and feature walls, which was extracted from the nearby Vals quarry.

The comprehensive program of refurbishment and expansion took more than two years to complete and was overseen by Bernerd and her team, who worked in conjunction with local architects Hauswirth Architekten. The new-build part of the project involved digging into the hillside to massively enlarge the ground floor area, while subtle work was undertaken within the original chalet to weave together the old and new structures seamlessly. Extensive space planning was carried out to ensure that the building's now 10,000 square feet fulfilled every accommodation requirement: a master bedroom suite, five additional suites, three staff bedrooms, an open-plan drawing/dining room, a family billiard room, a gym, a wine cellar, and a 650-square-foot kitchen. In addition, the site features pure skiing luxury: a private mountain tunnel entrance connecting the chalet to the slopes, the corridor of which was given a stunning, unexpectedly modern feel.

Throughout the chalet's rooms, the goal of the design was to eclectically "combine the old with the new, and introduce a warm palette." This goal was achieved by incorporating beautiful fabrics by Etro and Pierre Frey, combined with stylish contemporary yet classical furniture designed by Antonio Citterio and Poltrona Frau. The chalet also boasts an impressive art collection, including works by Howard Hodgkin, Tracey Emin, Rachel Howard, and Harland Miller—all of which have been placed to their best advantage, as has everything in this extraordinary mountain retreat.

Entrance with natural Vals stone walls

right: Artwork by Harland Miller, *Who Cares Wins*

# Villa in
# Sa Torre

LATITUDE: 39.5, LONGITUDE: 2.65

LOCATION: SA TORRE, PALMA DE MALLORCA, SPAIN

CLIENT: PRIVATE

COMPLETED: 2009

This cool and contemporary island retreat is located in the Sa Torre area of Mallorca and boasts spectacular uninterrupted sea views across the Bay of Palma toward the distant coastline of North Africa. Set within a private estate populated with gnarled olive trees and pink-blossomed almonds, the 15,000-square-foot new-build villa enjoys outstanding vistas of the Mediterranean coast thanks to its enormous windows and cleverly shaded terraces.

The client, who is an author, wanted a place where he and his wife could entertain friends and family, but also a space that could provide a haven for him to write his books amid peaceful, inspiring surroundings. From the outset, Bernerd and her former partner Thomas Griem worked with their team to provide creative direction, overseeing the complete design and build, from initial concept development through construction and completion. Their aim while working with a firm of local architects was to create a contemporary building that embodied a strong Mallorcan flavor.

Knowing the island well, Bernerd was thoroughly versed in the vernacular building style and thus able to reference it elegantly. The use of local materials, including sandstone blocks from the nearby quarry in Santanyi, was key in creating a building that would settle into the environment. The outside and inside spaces were designed so that there is virtually no physical division between them, with substantial windows on all three sides of the main living area looking out onto the landscaped gardens, effectively bringing the outside in. This effect is reinforced on the interior through the use of Santanyi stone cladding in some rooms. The locally quarried material not only looks dramatic and is location sympathetic, but it also helps keep the house cool in summer and warm in winter. Understanding the requirements of a hot climate, Bernerd ensured that the home offered ample shaded and decked patio areas, thus extending the living areas into the garden.

The villa's plan is fundamentally three large modernist glass boxes linked via interconnecting corridors, with the owner's writing room set on a rocky outcrop overlooking the endless blue sea. The contemporary feel is imbued with warmth, offsetting a predominately light and natural palette—demonstrated by dove gray walls and palest cream linens—with rich dark-wood flooring and paneling.

Ultimately requiring more than three years to complete, the project saw Bernerd and her team involved in every detail, for they had been given an open brief by the client from the get-go. The result is a modern yet thoroughly Mallorcan property, one that sensitively reflects a unique sense of place.

'The Writing Room'

# Marco Grill

LATITUDE: 51.4, LONGITUDE: -0.1

LOCATION: STAMFORD BRIDGE, FULHAM ROAD, FULHAM, LONDON, UK
CLIENT: CHELSEA FOOTBALL CLUB/MARCO PIERRE WHITE
COMPLETED: 2007

The chairman of Chelsea Football Club wanted to team up London's top restaurateur with London's top interior designer to create a new destination eatery at the club's famous Stamford Bridge home ground. As a result, Tara Bernerd & Partners was commissioned to work closely with Michelin-starred chef Marco Pierre White. They decided from the outset to create a brasserie with a modern edge that would "take dining at the football ground to a new level." This chic and classic destination restaurant occupies 2,000 square feet, yet it possesses a notable warmth and intimacy thanks to clever space planning, which includes the use of circular boothlike padded-leather banquettes that cocoon diners wanting a more private dining experience. The deluxe finishes also project an intentionally seductive quality, with statement pieces such as the cognac Swarovski crystal column and the black-and-white Italian floor mosaic inlaid at the center of the room adding a touch of allure. Likewise, the mirrored ceiling visually opens the space and reinforces a stylish '70s retro feel. The textile palette of warm grays and dark moss similarly adds a touch of sophisticated glamour to the otherwise predominately monochrome scheme. Crucial to the overall effect, the warm low-level lighting was designed to set a moody, seductive tone that complements the design and enhances the restaurant's intimate ambience. Like so many of Bernerd's projects, it is the careful and refined detailing that gives this space such an elegant and contemporary aesthetic.

# HighCliff

LATITUDE: 22.2, LONGITUDE: 114.1

LOCATION: STUBBS ROAD, THE PEAK, HONG KONG
CLIENT: HIGHCLIFF
COMPLETED: 2010

Because of Hong Kong's high land values, the "Pearl of the Orient," as it is sometimes called, has more pencil-thin skyscrapers than anywhere in the world. Among these, and by far the most celebrated in terms of design is HighCliff, a 73-story residential tower located on The Peak and set on the southern slope of Hong Kong's Happy Valley. Standing at 828 feet, it is one of the tallest residential buildings in the world and has been nicknamed by locals "The Chopsticks" because of its extremely slender double-ellipse twin-tower profile. Sitting atop this iconic building is a remarkable penthouse designed by Tara Bernerd and her team, led by Thomas Griem and Alex Hutchison. It occupies the entire floor plate and boasts a 360-degree view of Hong Kong. This super-deluxe yet surprisingly understated 3,500-square-foot apartment is all about intelligent space planning, ensuring a considered flow between areas. Quality materials—oak, bronze, sandstone, marble, onyx—were used in a way that brings their intrinsic material properties to the fore. The open-plan living area was broken up into distinct zones, each with its "own special mood and raison d'être." The overall palette is natural and muted, yet in true TB&P style sudden splashes of rich color give a sense of mood, whether an aubergine velvet sofa or an amber-hued ashtray. And as ever, it is the careful composition of elements—from the walls to the furniture to the books—that makes this project so visually unified and pleasing to the eye.

Artwork by Hong Hao

Artwork by Chen Jiagang

# Center Parcs Lodges & Treehouses

LATITUDE: 53.2, LONGITUDE: -1.08

LOCATION: NATIONWIDE, UK
CLIENT: CENTER PARCS / BLACKSTONE
COMPLETED: 2007–2011

As part of a major program of revitalization, Center Parcs ran a nationwide competition to transform its lodges and holistically support the brand overhaul across the UK. Tara Bernerd & Partners won the commission and subsequently an enormous rollout began of discreet, design-led Woodland Lodges, with Sherwood Forest being used to demonstrate the very first prototype cabins. Because of her background in real estate and track record within hospitality design, Bernerd was ideally placed to create simple yet stylish design-led accommodations within the tight budgetary constraints of what is in effect a family "cabin-style" destination. Using open-plan layouts, each lodge boasts not only a wood-burning stove, oak-style flooring, and wood paneling but also large windows overlooking the forest, thereby bringing a sense of the outdoors inside. For furnishings, Bernerd kept it simple by using modern neutral sofas and chairs, colorful striped rugs, and custom-made beds dressed with fresh white linen. Additional touches included a blackboard in the small stainless steel kit kitchens and wall-sized photographic murals, which add that all-important homey feel. Crucially, Bernerd demonstrated that beautiful contemporary design within the hospitality sector does not have to be the preserve of five-star boutiques or hotel grand dames. With clever and careful design and space planning, good design can be made more affordable.

# Westminster Terrace Penthouse

LATITUDE: 22.4, LONGITUDE: 114.1

LOCATION: TING KAU, TSUEN WAN, NEW TERRITORIES, HONG KONG

CLIENT: GROSVENOR ASIA / ASIA STANDARD

COMPLETED: 2010

Artworks by Steve Schapiro and Jim Lee (right)

When Tara Bernerd was approached by Nick Loup of Grosvenor Asia to design this luxury penthouse in a new development comprising 59 duplex apartments in Hong Kong, she saw it as an opportunity to explore a more contemporary interior architectural layout and indeed design. In addition, the style paid homage to the fact that in Hong Kong there has always been an appetite for something "a little more glitzy and glamorous." For this penthouse, with its panoramic views overlooking Kowloon and Hong Kong Island, Bernerd created an Eastern influenced, loft-style home. A striking art collection was curated by Hamiltons Gallery and Ben Brown Fine Arts, who worked closely with Bernerd throughout.

With a floor area of 7,000 square feet, this spacious penthouse is split over two levels, with the lower floor designed as an entirely open-plan space (unusual for Hong Kong). The lower-level space was cleverly segmented into three distinct interconnecting zones: the salon, dining room/kitchen, and drawing room, providing a suite of rooms for both living and entertaining. On the floor above, the number of bedrooms was reduced to just three so that each could have a large bathroom and the master suite its own private study. One of the main anchoring features of the penthouse is its amazing staircase, whose polished onyx treads are lit from within and produce a soft yellow-amber glow. The staircase functions as a focal point within the apartment and provides a stunning optical illusion, appearing to float freely in front of the double-height wall of stacked, locally quarried slate.

The skillful use of color and texture throughout the home adds a dramatic touch to the overall interior scheme. Colors range from the magenta screen dividing the kitchen and dining area, to the bespoke dark walnut shelving with its beautiful book-matched graining in the upstairs study, to the gleaming white and gray Italian marble walls in the master bathroom. There is also a strong sense of geometric dynamism within the scheme, thanks not only to the staircase but also to the way the overhead lighting has been cleverly handled in the corridor linking the dining area to the other rooms on the lower floor. Its orange-hued rectangular cut-out recesses bathe the rooms in a warm glow of ambient light. Perhaps most surprising about the apartment is its terrace and rooftop swimming pool, with considered treatment of these outdoor areas helping to extend the living space.

Throughout this project, one is struck by the exquisite combination of different materials, colors, and textures, all of which coalesce in a super-deluxe yet warm feeling. The expert use of "pooling" spotlights further enhances these different design elements. This, combined with a keen eye for details—the carefully selected books, glassware, candles, trays, blankets, and so on—has transformed an expansive space into an intimate home.

Artwork by Erwin Olaf

Artwork by Jim Lee and Guido Mocafico (right)

Artwork by Irving Penn:
*Iceland Poppy (H)*, New York, 2006

Artwork by Irving Penn:
*Iceland Poppy (H)*, New York, 2006

Hallway with artwork by Candida Höfer

Artwork by Irving Penn:
*Ranunculus 'Picotee'*, New York, 2006

Artworks by Tseng Kwong Chi

# Belgraves

LATITUDE: 51.4, LONGITUDE: -0.1

LOCATION: CHESHAM PLACE, BELGRAVIA, LONDON, UK
CLIENT: THOMPSON HOTELS / HARILELA GROUP
COMPLETED: 2012

A stone's throw from her office in Hans Street, Belgraves
was one of Tara Bernerd's earlier projects in the boutique
hotel market and ultimately became the springboard to
numerous other hotel commissions. The design DNA for
Belgraves was the brainchild of Bernerd, who worked
closely with Aron Harilela and the founder of Thompson
Hotels, Jason Pomeranc, both of whom shared a similar
vision for the type of experience that hotels should offer
guests. The extant structure had huge potential, with
its prestigious location in Belgravia, just minutes from
Knightsbridge, Hyde Park, and Sloane Square. Yet,
transforming this former Sheraton hotel built in the
1970s into Thompson Hotels' London flagship was no
small undertaking. In fact, scaffolding covered the facade
for over a year as the team's vision took shape behind the
hoardings. The full interior architecture and design of
this project called for not only innovative spatial planning
of all the layouts—from the ground-floor lobby to the
restaurant, bar, and library—but also the refurbishment
of 85 suites and bedrooms. Bernerd worked hand in hand
with the project architects, EPR Architects, and offered
creative direction on the building's exterior treatment as
well. Using a variety of rich and tactile finishes, including
Arabescato marble, smoked-wood flooring, graystone,
brick walls, and smoked glass, Bernerd aimed to create a
stylish, warm, and moody "place" that would channel a
loftlike residential feel, thereby giving guests the feeling
of inhabiting "an original home in the heart of Belgravia."
Crucially for the client, Bernerd and her team were able to
articulate through this project the attitude and flavor of
Thompson Hotels and Harilela's innate style.

# Present

CF: *We've talked about what design was like when you first started out. Now I'd like to step into the present and ask how you think design is perceived today.*

TB: Certainly the Internet and sites like Pinterest have made people far more aware of design and help inform their design choices. Today, we are able to get a lot more information about design much faster than ever before, and that has boosted our expectations about how places should be designed. I remember as a really young girl growing up in England when restaurants were still pretty dull places. Now London is one of the most incredible global go-to cities. You only have to walk around Shoreditch or Berkeley Square, or whichever borough of London you're in, and at your fingertips are an array of amazing restaurant experiences—not just the food but the interiors, too. I get a lot of inspiration from the design of restaurants, some by people I work with and some by other designers. I think increasingly design is being seen as a necessary part of everything we touch. And as the role of design grows, the more that people can take from it.

*Do you think there is an increasing convergence between design and other creative disciplines? For example, you must be taking inspiration not only from the realm of design but also from the worlds of art, fashion, music, film. Do you do this consciously or subconsciously?*

It is definitely subconscious. I can get an idea for a design from all sorts of things. Sometimes I get an inspiration and just park it in my mind, holding on to it until it is relevant to a new project. Everyone looks for a set of rules, how to create something; for me, I have to be open to inspiration from all areas of life. The creative industries can be difficult to fathom, and I've often had to rely on instinct layered with experience. I try to feel what's right for a given project, as opposed to what everyone else is looking for or doing.

*Do you think the role of today's hotels is to transcend day-to-day reality?*

Although hotels are today's lifestyle palaces because of their scale, they also play the role of home away from home for most of the people staying in them. People need to have a rooted feeling, a sense of place, so as a designer you need to be sincere to where you are, which means being sympathetic to the climate and the culture. A way of creating a sense of place is by bringing in layers. It might be books, it might be a mixture of objects that you collect, but it is those final touches that give an interior that crucial sense of character. I often approach the design of a hotel as though it was my own home, but a very big one. So its entrance is my hallway, and I will make the entrance doors feel special so there is a sense of welcome and presence. As I bring people in, depending on the location, there might be a fireplace that they make their way around before they get to the front desk or the concierge. And then we'll create an area for socializing, which could be like the place where you'd have relaxing drinks in your own drawing room or study. We also try to create seductive little areas that cocoon the user.

*Presumably what you are trying to do above all else is emotionally connect people to the space. Do you have in your mind's eye the type of person who is going to inhabit this space? And when you are working with private clients, do you tailor interiors to their tastes or interests?*

As interior architectural designers we have not worked with that many private clients out of choice, but the ones we have collaborated with include some high-profile individuals. We find that often people don't know precisely what they want, so they come to us for a vision. Because of how we work, we have a strong signature or sense of place, so we try to guide the client. The same applies to the development projects. With the hotel projects, invariably the hotelier makes strong initial inputs but

Portrait by Jason Alden

goes along with our visions and then looks to us to push the boundaries.

*Good design always stems from the realization that design can make a difference. In Scandinavia there is a belief that good design is the birthright of all. I think that is such a key philosophy—that whether you are designing a hotel room or an apartment, you are essentially helping to enhance people's daily lives.*

I really uphold that belief and subscribe to the idea that you are where you live, because it is such an essential part of one's existence. When I used to do interviews, I'd often be asked my top tips for interiors. Because not everyone has a budget, the first thing I'd say is, tidy up your house, edit, throw out stuff, make sure it's clean. Even if you just have one room to live in, rather than a flat or a house, if you make sure it's organized and tidy, it will make you feel better. If you oxygenate that emotion and put it over a home or hotel, it means that from the moment you arrive it seeps into you, because our moods are enormously influenced by the quality of our surroundings.

*Although a lot of your hotels are at the high end of affordability, you have also worked on projects that are more democratic in their reach, such as Center Parcs. I remember you saying once that was one of the projects of which you were proudest.*

I loved that project. It doesn't make any difference to me whether I'm doing a Four Seasons hotel or designing a lodge for Center Parcs, I care about getting it right and still apply the same rules. The first thing that matters is asking the questions: What are these places meant to be? Who are they for? What is their DNA? Where are they? Are we on the beach and looking at blue skies and golden sands, or are we in Sherwood Forest? From these questions the truth about the project surfaces, and from there we can design appropriately.

*Do you like the constraints of working within budgets?*

We always work within budgets. It's a myth to think the Center Parcs job was any more budget driven than a hotel for Four Seasons. It's just that some of our clients want to create super-deluxe schemes for a very high-end audience. But there's no way any of these projects would be commercially viable if we didn't use all our design savviness to create them according to secured budgets. So the budgets might differ, but we are always value engineering.

*Yes, it is extraordinary how international and democratic design has become.*

In that regard, I think Ikea has been an unbelievable influence, and I'm a huge fan of what they do. I'm as passionate about them as I am about Phillips De Pury auction house. Look at all the beautiful furniture coming out of Italy, too. There is endless choice, and people want help with those choices.

*And that's where you come in.*

Today, it is okay to say, "How do I edit this?" Whereas before it was, "Oh, I don't need a designer; I can do it myself." That's why the design industry is now a viable career choice. People have woken up to the fact that just as they'd hire a professional to help with their finances or administer to their health, they can hire a professional for advice on making their homes better. It's an important career that can have a profound effect on the quality of our lives.

*Would you describe yourself as a maximalist? By that I mean, are you the antithesis of a minimalist? Do you always want homey warmth rather than a stark coolness?*

Not necessarily, because I could do the opposite. A room could be about having a resin floor with a really chic bed, a single chair, and just one book. I essentially self-edit. I like what an accessory can do to a room after we've built it, and I like what an accessory can do to a person. You can wear the plainest white suit, and just your glasses might say enough and be all you need.

*In terms of how you place things, do you find the perfect spot for something and then it just stays there forever?*

Yes. I'm a nightmare. A client I'm currently designing for in New York asked me to do his home in London a couple of years ago, and I swear I could go in after not having been in there for a year and be able to move every book back to exactly where I left it. In my apartment, I know where everything sits, literally to the angle of the ashtrays, so if I come back and someone has moved my books, I'll know. It's the same in my office. So yes, I'll often choose something quickly using my creative instinct, but then I'll take a long time to site it, and then it is there forever. But it's one thing in your own home; it is a totally different matter in a hotel, where you leave it absolutely perfect at the end of a project, but then things inevitably get moved or changed over time. The original vision may be diluted. When we completed SIXTY SoHo, it was absolutely perfect down to the smallest detail. Luckily Jason Pomeranc, whom we worked with on this project, understood the importance of keeping it the way it was. He is one of those rare and brilliant hoteliers who are visionaries and can see how people want to live and be. All my projects are like my children—you can't be a total control freak, but there are times when I go back to a project and things have been moved or changed and I just have to sit there. Then again, I've been known to move a lamp back to where it should be whilst people are having drinks at Belgraves. It has happened.

*I'm sure it has.*

I see the same with a lot of my friends working in the restaurant business. They might be chatting with me but they are not fully there because they're clocking what's going on around them. Then suddenly they get up, move a table, take an order, and then they come back and sit down. Because they've done "it," they can then relax and engage again. That's how it goes in my world, too.

*Certainly the eclectic mixing thing that you do gives a strong sense of home. I always think that when an interior is mono-styled, say with an art deco theme, it just looks artificial. Likewise, interiors done in a minimalist style can look contrived. Whereas you draw references from all sorts of places—mixing contemporary design with midcentury-modern objects with cutting-edge avant-garde art. Do you think it is that mélange of different things which enables you to create that all-important homey quality?*

I don't know; it is so difficult to deconstruct one's approach because it has become such an intuitive thing, but there are certain stock points that really count with me that I can see reflected in all the different types of projects I've worked on. For example, before I'd even consider adding a book or a Murano ashtray, we would look at the overall design as though there was no color or finish at all. Initially, it is only about the layout, and that is fundamentally where everything starts. It is a question of whether I'm opening a door to a two-bed lodge in Sherwood Forest, or I'm opening the door to my suite in the Four Seasons, or walking into the lobbies of Thompson Chicago or the new Thompson Hollywood we're working on now. Everything is about feeling the space and working out how one can make it work the way it needs to. Another thing to consider is if we have open plan: do we have cocooned areas, and if so, where do people sit? Once those layout decisions are established, it doesn't matter if I cover the walls in stone, wood, or paint. It isn't until the layout is in place that we look at palette and "spec." I think probably the best way to explain spec, or specification, is if you had a doll's house and tipped it upside down, then the spec would be everything that's left behind. It's our floors, our ceilings, our walls.

So that's the first palette the design starts with. It's here that you'll have the wood come into play, or you might have cork

on the ceiling. The next step is starting to look at the interior fabrics, which are a second palette. You need to make sure that your second palette sits with the first. Then we start the layering process, but at this stage we wouldn't be considering any of the details, like books or vases, because we haven't even got the furniture in the game.

*So your design is like an artist's palette that you're building up.*

Yes, we layer it. But instead of peeling an onion, we make them. You could say we essentially build onions!

*This layering process is your methodology and must ultimately be the reason your interiors have such a distinctive look despite being so diverse.*

This process is extremely important to me. That's why I'm not particularly keen on going into a home that's already been done, which I'm sometimes asked to do, and help finish it by putting out books and bits, because that's not true. However, what you're saying about a look or style is right. One of the things about the design world is that people like to label you, and it's hard to describe yourself and what you do in those terms. It's safe to say that I'm not a chintzy girl. Although I have very feminine sides to me, our work is often described as more masculine. Sometimes I think our look is a bit androgynous. As much as women seduce men, men seduce women. So something smoky and sexy and handsome doesn't alienate women. And it is more in my nature to go for an incredible iron that could be, say, used for a Crittall door, mixed with wood and concrete and a fantastic gray flannel . . . Everything I've described is about the furthest thing from what most people think of as being feminine, but those are my natural inclinations.

*I also get the feeling that you like using materials that have real integrity and quality. And it's not only the quality of the wood or tiles but also how beautifully they've been laid. The rawness of materials seems important to you. Often with interior designers, what they do is all about surface show, whereas you seem far more interested in the nuts and bolts of constructing an interior and that, throughout the process, you're building in a sense of quality.*

I think quality or workmanship is paramount. We can have the concept, the vision, we can draw out the floor plans, we can draw out the elevations, we can add spec and finish and style and concept, but once that is handed over, our detailed drawings and the schematics are key to realizing everything. On all projects, you have to stay on top of everything because the construction, deliverables, and workmanship are all vital. This means that the detailed drawing packages and FF&E—furniture, fixtures, and equipment—schedules that leave our office are like bibles, ensuring everything is in place and delivered. That is a whole other side of the job that no one sees.

*You're currently working on the new development, One Park Drive, for which Herzog & De Meuron is the lead architect. Who are the other architects you've found a good synergy with?*

When working with such high-profile architectural firms as Herzog & de Meuron, we really get into the nitty-gritty of the building's interior layouts. In fact, we become the "train spotters" of the internal spaces, which is an integral role. The interior layout might not be as relevant to the lead architects, who have their hands full building a landmark, but it can make the difference of a million pounds per unit to the seller. We get into that layout and start asking the questions that will help sell it: Do we want an open-plan kitchen? How should that kitchen work? We are interior architects working far more in the box, and we never profess to be anything else.

I'm a huge fan of contemporary architecture, and have always been influenced by it far more than what's going on in interior design, which is why you see a lot of that exterior industrial feel in my designs. But we don't encroach on the role of the "star-architect"; rather, we support it. We say to the other side, "We have as much belief in what you're doing as you do, but it needs to be continued on the inside of the building." As a result, we have good relationships with all the architects we've worked with. They like how we have that interior architectural approach and an understanding of the building's architectural DNA. Therefore a cozy sitting room isn't cozy because of the books we've put in it, but because of how that room has been oriented and shaped.

*I think you once described your partnership team as the Navy Seals of the interior design world. It seems that being a well-coordinated team is essential to what you do.*

For a big part of my life, I really wanted to go into film, and I even went to film school for a bit. Interior design and architecture are comparable to the film business because nobody really stands out or matters unless everybody stands out and matters. Whether you're designing a building and its interior or making a movie, it takes a mass of creative people, each with different roles, creating something together. Likewise, at the end of the process, you have to deliver on time and on budget and make a show that people want to go and see.

At all times, it can't be your ego that drives it. But like a film director, you infuse a project with your taste and style. The star of our show might be a wood wall featuring a Gio Ponti armchair, as opposed to Brad Pitt and Angelina Jolie. It's about not just the layers of the design process, but a constant respect for the fact that this happens only because of the work that goes on behind it. Maintaining a good relationship with the owner-developer is also crucial to a project's success because they, too, will have ideas that need to be incorporated. We don't just sit and do this for a couple of months; each design requires a couple of years of our lives, which means that relationships need to be strong to endure the course of the projects, along with their inevitable ups and downs.

*On a hotel project, how long does it usually take from start to finish?*

How long is a piece of string! If they're good and they work on time, it's about two years of design.

*Does everything evolve design-wise over that two-year period, or do you know from the start how everything will look at the end, so you just hunker down and get on with it?*

Oh, we know. We come up with the picture at the start, and it all follows on from there. Everything runs years ahead, so we have to be highly attuned to a vision from the outset.

*So, the reality is, you are always living in the future?*

Yes, I live in the future and I live in different worlds. I'm very happy in my office with my team, but my head never turns off. You're creating these conceptual worlds that you live in. You live in the future because not only are you designing for the future, but once a job ends, you need to have another one lined up to flow seamlessly into. Though I can't bring it in too soon because we're too busy with the job in hand.

*It sounds like there's a lot of balancing. Not only that, but from the start of discussions with a client to the final "Yes, we want to go ahead with you" stage, you must undertake a colossal amount of preparation and work.*

Of course! A lot of work is for presentations and pitches and discussions. There are huge highs when things fall into place, but also disappointments when we don't win a commission. The one thing I would say is that, when you're as passionate as I am about what you do, of course it's a hit when you don't win a pitch. But it's an unbelievable high when you do. Even when you don't get a job you really want, you have to keep moving. Although I don't brush off disappointments, I do feel that it is the synergy with the clients we've worked with that is one of the biggest keys to success, probably more than our design work. Because, if they understand your vision and give you the support to see it through, then it will work. If there's someone who doesn't want to work with us, we might be disappointed because we love the project, but we understand that the pitching process is a bit like dating. If that person doesn't want to be with you, don't push it. But if they do, you will get so much more out of the relationship.

*While working on projects that span years, you must eventually build up a mutual trust. When a client trusts you implicitly, it must make the job so much easier.*

It is a big responsibility.

*It must be, because things could go wrong so easily, given the nature and scale of the projects you undertake.*

Of course, sometimes things don't go exactly according to plan, but I think my clients know that every project really matters to me. I don't take what they give me lightly. It doesn't mean that problems won't arise, but I think our work is characterized by integrity and truth. That has really set us apart, and it doesn't matter whether our style is more industrial, bold or handsome, chic-edgy, or however people describe it, there is a sincerity in our process. That's how we work in the present, and that's how I intend to continue working into the future.

# Apartment in Central Park West

LATITUDE: 40.7, LONGITUDE: -73.9

LOCATION: CENTRAL PARK WEST, NEW YORK CITY, NEW YORK, USA

CLIENT: PRIVATE

COMPLETED: 2013

This 2,000-square-foot apartment enjoys breathtaking
views over "The City That Never Sleeps." Its location
within a landmark tower, however, meant that Bernerd,
along with partner Nicola Watkins and their team, had
to be highly creative in terms of space planning to adhere
to the relatively restrictive remodeling guidelines already
in place. By carefully delineating definable living zones,
they were able to orient the layout to provide the most
comfortable and functional suite of rooms within the
building's existing framework. For this project, Bernerd
also provided a complete interior design package, which
included an array of luxury finishes, such as book-matched
walnut for the specially designed built-in bookcase/
diversion station, high-quality leather for the feature walls
in both the living room and master bedroom, and art
glass set within the stunning screen that partially divides
the dining area and lobby. The client, an avid collector
of contemporary fine art, owned key pieces that worked
spectacularly well with the scheme. While the apartment
was designed to be the perfect setting for entertaining,
it was also thoughtfully conceived for daily living, too.
Bernerd took care to provide intimate cocooning areas for
when the client is home alone, such as the small dining
nook off the kitchen, where the owner loves to sit every
morning while having breakfast and taking in the superb
view overlooking Central Park.

The study.
All artwork from the client's personal collection.

# MY
# Orient Star

LATITUDE: 40.0, LONGITUDE: 28.9

LOCATION: ISTANBUL, TURKEY

CLIENT: PRIVATE

COMPLETED: 2013

The *Orient Star* is a 47-meter (154-foot) superyacht that
Bernerd, together with Michelle Hughes, Stephanie
Weatherly, and the TB&P team, was involved in designing
from the outset, working in close collaboration with the
builder CMB Yachts, a marine shipyard based in Antalya,
Turkey. Bernerd not only devised with her team a full
interior layout to accommodate up to ten guests, but
she also provided a complete interior design package.
The resulting interiors, spread over three decks, display
Bernerd's understanding of the owners as a family and
how they liked to spend their time while afloat. To
accommodate large gatherings, the decks were designed
with an expansive seating area for alfresco dining, while
the main salon is truly a stunning space for entertaining.
Private cocooning spaces were also cleverly incorporated
within the design, and a careful focus was given to the
execution of the various fixtures and fittings, such as the
exquisite embossed leather handrails. As Bernerd notes,
when you are designing a yacht, "it is not about thinking
outside the box, but making a world within the box." It is
the team's careful consideration of even the most intricate
details from the beginning of the design process that
imbues this luxurious vessel with its unique character and
superior comfort.

Artwork by Elger Esser. © DACS 2016

# Thompson Chicago

LATITUDE: 41.9, LONGITUDE: -87.6

LOCATION: EAST BELLEVUE PLACE, CHICAGO, ILLINOIS, USA
CLIENT: THOMPSON HOTELS / A J CAPITAL / WALTON ST CAPITAL
COMPLETED: 2013

Thompson Chicago is a downtown boutique hotel set amid the historic mansions and tree-lined streets of Chicago's famed Gold Coast. Located right next to the iconic Gibsons Bar & Steakhouse and within the hip Golden Triangle district, the buzziest neighborhood of the city during summer, Thompson Chicago was Tara Bernerd & Partners' second project for the Thompson Group. It was also the office's first major hotel project undertaken stateside. A significantly larger project than Belgraves, the earlier hotel Bernerd had done for Thompson, this hotel had nearly three times the guest accommodation: 247 bedrooms and suites. In addition to devising the layouts and interior design for these spaces, Bernerd was responsible for the full interior architecture and design of all the building's public areas, including two bars and a restaurant, Nico Osteria, for the renowned Chicago restaurateurs One Off Hospitality.

The first thing Bernerd and partner Tommy Gymnander did on being hired was to analyze the floor plans with their team. The original configuration had a porte-cochère entrance, which was deemed a waste of prime space. They quickly realized that by eliminating this feature and substituting it with a glazed facade, the internal floor space of the building would increase considerably. The team also optimized the floor plate by removing a circular lift in the existing lobby. As Bernerd recalls, "The old hotel was a complete disaster, so we went in and ripped everything out and reevaluated the interior language." This language was loft luxury meets urban industrial chic, with reverential nods to the architecture of Frank Lloyd Wright, including the sculptural bar clad in brass tubing, towering two-tone brick columns, and overall rich, vibrant palette. Warm elements, such as bespoke millwork using American woods and luxurious velvets and leathers, also helped set the mood, as did the construction of a welcoming fireplace in the lobby. Another key feature of the design is a sweeping staircase linking the lobby to an elevated gallery, which then leads to the restaurant, whose design incorporates various private dining spaces. Bernerd consciously infused the public areas with a strong been-there-forever character by introducing beams, wall paneling, and glazed tiles, all of which help evoke a strong sense of place while retaining a worldly, eclectic sensibility.

Lobby salon walls curated by Indiewalls. Featured artists include Sasha Andruzheychik, Elana Baziz, Dan Bina, Malcolm Brown, Dan Harries, Daniel Oglander, Annie Terrazzo, Craig Tinsky, Robert Whitman.

Artwork by Wes Lang (left) and Cynthia Daignault.
Image courtesy Exhibition A

# SIXTY
# SoHo

LATITUDE: 40.7, LONGITUDE: -74.0

LOCATION: THOMPSON STREET, SOHO, NEW YORK CITY, NY, USA

CLIENT: SIXTY HOTELS

COMPLETED: 2014

SIXTY SoHo is representative of Tara Bernerd's commercial oeuvre, a fact she attributes to the great synergy she enjoys with its owners, the Pomeranc family. Thanks to their shared vision, Bernerd was able to put her "home-away-from-home" philosophy of hotel design into thrilling practice. The resulting interiors are pure TB&P style—handsome, but with attitude, thanks to a material palette of glass, tile, concrete, and wood.

Having sold the Thompson hotel group, the Pomerancs were looking to create a flagship for their new hotel chain, SIXTY. For this iconic building located at 60 Thompson Street, in New York's fashionable SoHo area, Bernerd was asked to oversee a complete design overhaul, alongside partners Nicola Watkins and Stephanie Weatherly. The hotel's floor plan was entirely reconfigured, transforming the lobby spaces and creating The Gordon Bar, with John McDonald and Mercer Street Hospitality. In addition, the hotel's 96 bedrooms and suites were completely redesigned. Scattered throughout the public areas are contemporary artworks from Jason Pomeranc's personal collection, which add to the modern and sophisticated aesthetic. In fact, art punctuates most of the hotel, and Bernerd and Weatherly worked closely with Jason Pomeranc to curate a collection that enhanced the hotel's vibe of understated luxe. Bernerd also introduced White Cube, the contemporary art gallery in London, and their artist Harland Miller, to Pomeranc and the team, commissioning a unique series of sketches and studies for each of the guest bedrooms. Complementing the art are carefully chosen furniture, rugs, and lighting, all of which gives these spaces a homey quality. Perhaps the biggest transformation, however, was visually opening up the lobby areas by adding massive floor-to-ceiling Crittall windows that bring typical Manhattan vistas into play. Upstairs, the bedrooms are best described as minimalist with a chic twist: cream walls with leather-padded headboards, stylish Italian midcentury-style floor lights, and petrol-blue velvet sofas and cushions. The most popular areas in the hotel have proved to be the light-filled Gordons Bar, with its stunning geometric tiled floor, and the art-lined lobby lounge, whose wonderful mix of objets d'art and books would make anyone feel at home.

Artwork by Harland Miller: *The Next Life's On Me*, 2012

# Treehouse Hotel at Port Lympne

LATITUDE: 51.0, LONGITUDE: 1.0

LOCATION: PORT LYMPNE RESERVE, ASHFORD, KENT, UK

CLIENT: ASPINALL FOUNDATION

COMPLETED: 2015

IMPORTANT NOTICE
FOR OUR GUESTS

Adult presence at all times
with young children
is compulsory on the
Terrace / Balcony

For this project, Bernerd worked closely with the chairman of the Aspinall Foundation, Damian Aspinall, to interpret his vision for a treehouse retreat in Port Lympne, Kent. Sited on a curving ridge and cantilevered into the tree canopy high above the Aspinall family's 600-acre wild animal reserve, the Treehouse Hotel offers luxury that is both minimalist and chic. Each of the hotel's ten self-catering suites is fronted by glass and has its own private balcony for the all-important act of viewing the "wild": —the reserve is home to over 88 species and 700 animals, including lions, zebras, giraffes, and black rhinoceros. For each of the suites, Bernerd and her partners Michelle Hughes and Stephanie Weatherly created two double bedrooms, a bathroom, a sleek kitchen/diner, and a lounging area that is simple yet comfortable. Intended first and foremost as a get-away-from-it-all natural retreat, the hotel incorporates a muted palette of creams and grays that gives it a restful quality. The use of wood-plank feature walls also helps to evoke an entirely appropriate cabin-in-the-woods feel. Achieved within a relatively limited budget, this project demonstrates the ability of Tara Bernerd & Partners to create stylishly contemporary places without needing to resort to the use of luxury finishes. For instance, the double-belt feature on the headboards and the little polished-concrete-topped tables in the kitchen/dining areas give a sense of cutting-edge style, yet neither element was particularly costly. Indeed, it is this innovative attention to detail that enhances the overall look of the suites, creating the perfect setting for a treetop escape.

# Future

CF: *You once said to me that you feel like you are perpetually living in the future, which I can thoroughly understand since you are always working on projects that are on the near to far horizon in terms of delivery.*

TB: Apart from the day-to-day demands of running the business, you have to continuously look ahead while working on the next projects. You are not only designing something that has to stand the test of time, but also something that might well be launched several years ahead. It's all about forward thinking, but I'm not unique in this respect. Friends of mine who are magazine editors often have to live months ahead before the issue they're working on comes out. The same can be found in the fashion world, with designers having to prepare collections way ahead of their shows. So I wouldn't claim to have some special magic touch. I do think you need a kind of predictive skill when working within the creative industries. But yes, mentally living in the future is part of my job description.

*Do you find this forward-looking aspect of your work exhilarating?*

I don't question it; you just have to live that way if you're doing what I do. Sometimes we all want to slow down and just live for the moment, but the sense of exhilaration you're talking about comes from being able to appreciate the present moment while also being able to live years ahead of yourself, too.

*Given how fast technology is evolving and changing our lifestyles, do you try to future-proof your projects? And if so, how?*

I believe the rapid change in technology will influence our lives dramatically. I would be foolish not to embrace it, yet I can't pretend I'm the savviest techno-head out there. I often talk at conferences, which gives me the opportunity to hear how other speakers think our lives will be changed by future technologies. The lifestyle shifts resulting from these technologies will inevitably have an impact on how we design. I'm not talking about projects that we're launching in two years' time; I'm talking about twenty years down the line. Will we need car parking spaces? What sorts of homes will need to be built? How are we going to be living day-to-day? I don't know if I'll live to see the world change so rapidly that we'll put on a VR headset or augmented-reality glasses and not even need our physical interiors because we have virtual ones. I believe 100 percent that anything is possible when it comes to the future. And because everything is constantly changing, I try to future-proof my projects by attempting to absorb, understand, and imagine how new technologies will affect us.

*You correctly predicted the advent of the "house dog" in hotels. In what other ways will future hotel interiors be able to create that crucial home-away-from-home vibe?*

The idea of the hotel house dog touched on the point that although hotel companies are first and foremost financial businesses, to succeed they need to connect with people's emotions. As people travel more and more, and our worlds are often no longer tied to one city, there is an increasing demand on hotels to be more like home. Therefore, the hoteliers have to inject a sense of emotion into what they do, and that's where we come in.

*How do you do that?*

Well, it's not about sticking one's thumb in the air and seeing where the creative winds are blowing or relying only on an instinctive hunch; it's about due diligence. It's about analyzing what has worked, and what isn't working. What are people warming to? Where are people naturally going when they travel? Then we study this type of information—it's a science. We listen to people, we read the statistical feedback from all the hotel groups we work with, so that we can understand the cultural climate we're working in.

After you've correlated all these data, plus mixed in some

Portrait by Graciela Cattarossi

instinct, of course, you see that it's this sense of home away from home that most people seemingly want. Yes, there are different categories of travelers. Some will not want this kind of experience. They'll just want a capsule to stay in, and perhaps for others we'll be designing sterile pods.

The bigger hotels and the brands will also need to respond to this new and emerging desire. The bedroom has always been a place of sanctuary, and I don't think that is going to change, but what we want out of a bathroom has already radically altered. Today it can't be a throwaway little back room.

*Is there an example of a future project you're working on where you are consciously building in a sense of home?*

As you know, we're building a hotel here in Los Angeles, and next week we'll be presenting a lobby and its finishes that include concrete and white brick, which are very reminiscent of the 1970s. The scheme also combines tan leather with cantilevered gray concrete. But I know that despite having an industrial aesthetic, it will feel like somewhere one can recline and own. Maybe somewhere you might like to sit and read a newspaper, or use your laptop, as well as doubling as a lounge bar.

It's all about respecting one's own instinct for the future, but basing that instinct on observation. As the world gets more and more technologically driven, it is interesting to note that while everyone can work on a laptop anywhere, they are not choosing to sit in small white cellular offices to do so; instead they're choosing friendly open-plan spaces with big wooden tables or casual lobbies. The reason is that they want all that warmth around them, even while they're isolated in their own little cyberspaces. So it's up to us as designers and space planners to gauge how one can build a feeling of home into schemes, and how appropriate it is for any given project.

*Before you start designing a project, do you undertake a lot of background research into its cultural context?*

Of course. And the other thing that comes into play is the type of project. If we're building a home, that's one thing, or if we're building a hotel in a city, that's another thing; if we're building a resort, then it's something entirely different. So there isn't a list of formulae or rules that I can apply to all these types of projects, but for each project—large or small—you need to appreciate its context and understand the cultural values that lie behind it.

*As people become increasingly nomadic, do you think the concept of home will change even further? And if so, do you think that's why*

*people seem increasingly to want emotionally and culturally connective places rather than anonymous anywhere-in-the-world spaces?*

Absolutely, and I think that has been part of the success of things like Airbnb. I think people do want to connect. Travel is no longer just for the privileged and elite; travel is now part of many people's lives. Many people want where they are staying to have cultural context, but they also want comfort. It's like cooking—there are all these ingredients and you have to make them work together. So, yes, you need the indigenous flavor, but you also need internationally recognized standards of service.

*Given that you are constantly traveling, where do you feel is home?*

I used to struggle with answering that question until I realized that I don't really live anywhere because I keep moving about so much. And I don't know if today I could stay in one place permanently. However, I feel I am very alive in New York, as I do here, too.

*In terms of how digital technology is changing the way you work, you recently showed me a wonderful 3-D visualization of a project you're working on that allows one to effectively walk though an interior using an iPad. This type of technology is going to evolve, and it is not too much of a stretch to imagine clients looking at their commissioned projects wearing VR headsets in the next year or so. But I'm wondering whether technology such as this can get in the way of creative gut instinct, since you are creating an interior down to the smallest detail in the virtual realm before even the first proverbial brick is laid.*

We are increasingly using 3-D visualisation, but I remember years ago having a client who, although I didn't want to say anything, was obviously struggling to read a floor layout. Regardless of whatever technology is available, we've always drawn everything up, from early sketches that go into CAD layouts, which we then take into elevations and detailed sections. But not all of our clients can read these, so we would build models, and we still do and they are great. CGIs—computer-generated imagery—are essentially moving models on a screen. But there are still so many issues with them. I can't get the detail of the finishes and I can't get the warmth of a room, but I can't work without them anymore; they are our future. I don't just embrace CGI—I have a whole department dedicated to it, and it is growing. Hence why I have been brave enough to use some in this publication!

*When we first met, you mentioned people wearing VR headsets to experience interior design, and this technology is already being trialed in the industry. Do you see it quickly becoming mainstream?*

I'm sure that will happen. Why not? I'll get home and I'll have a perfect box and I could design all the different room layouts. I could put in contact lenses and I'll have TV-like walls with a kind of white-stone resin look, and I will click my eyes and I will see rooms that will feel like I'm living in them. And then I'll click my contact lenses again for a different look. Maybe I'll want a moodier smoky-club woody feel because its winter, and click, my house will be that. Why not? I don't think we can even imagine where it is going to go, but I hope to be a part of it if I am here.

*Do you think the way you pitch for a job will remain the same?*

I don't think there is any formula for pitching. It all comes from every architect or design firm doing it their own way. The way we pitch is that I tell a story—my story of a design vision—and it's my job to tell that story better than the other side.

*You've mentioned that in the future you would like to partner with other entities, namely developers and hoteliers, as an investor. Do you think that would allow you more creative freedom? And do you see it as a way to enable you to benefit more from all the work and added value you put into projects?*

Well, the future has moved rapidly since we last saw each other because I'm already talking to a hotelier about doing some work together. I don't necessarily want to start my own brand of hotels, but it is not something I'd rule out either. At the moment, however, that's not on the horizon. But what I'm very keen to do is continue taking the lead interior architectural designer role and then perhaps on occasion go in with the hotel owners as a joint venture partner. It is not that I would have more creative freedom, because I think we are already given enormous creative freedom just by being appointed for our ideas. What such a partnering arrangement would give me, however, is long-term protection of that product. It would mean that when I walk away, "said book" will not be moved, the lamps would be left exactly where they should be; it means that I can have more of a say in the candles, the music, the scent of a place, and in the service offered. Because if all of those other components don't work in a hotel, we are immediately faulted. With my passion for what I do, having skin in the game would be a way for me to ensure longer-term quality.

*I know you're planning to open an office in the United States, but have you thought about having an office elsewhere, say in Hong Kong, where your work has already been well received?*

We have had a satellite office in Hong Kong during projects, and we've been asked by our clients there to set up a permanent office, which I'm considering. In New York, we've seen a space that we're hoping to take. It's about being where I'm needed, not about massive global expansion. I like being very hands-on. So our London headquarters has twenty-five members but that's likely to increase to thirty. However, I don't want the office to get much bigger than that. Having a satellite office in the United States would enable me to be more hands-on with clients who are based here.

*If you'd had a crystal ball when you first started on your own back in 2002, would you have believed the types of projects you'd be working on now? What do you attribute your success to? Hard work? Talent? Luck?*

Probably all of those. Certainly the hard work of a talented team has been a major factor. Someone asked me the other evening whether we make our own luck, and I really don't know the answer to that. When I set up my company fifteen years ago, I had no idea that we'd be working on the kinds of projects we're now doing, but I do remember thinking that I would give it my damndest best shot. I hoped my best shot would get me somewhere, I just didn't know where it would be. I also have been blessed with incredible clients whom I will remain ever thankful to.

*I know this is a pretty stock-in-trade interview question, but I'm really interested in finding out, looking to the future, what your ultimate dream project would be. If you could have any project in the world, what would you most want to do?*

I'm doing it. You know, when you asked me about looking back to when I first started, some of the hotels we've worked on would have been my ultimate dream. Doing a monograph would have been another dream. But I think one of the main dreams, frankly, is that we're all still here and can keep going and doing more. I would like to think we could carry on making a mark in the hotel sector and resorts, and I think we have a strong touch on the projects we work on in residential developments, so I'd like to stay with that. I think as a team we're all extremely interested in partnering roles instead of just designing and handing over, but that's not a given. Also, I still love the creating of yachts, and there's hopefully more of those to come. It would be fun to do a really chic airplane soon— perhaps one of my own would be the real goal! I think there are certain countries that would be interesting to work in, too. Cuba, for instance, and Scandinavia interest me greatly.

*As I get older, the more I realize that the most important thing about life is people, not things or perceived status. I get the feeling you've known this for a while, and that is why your interiors are designed from such a strong human-centric perspective. They seem to me to be thoughtfully conceived as places for people to happily inhabit, rather than grandiose statement spaces. Is this the underlying truth behind what you do? Is it a question of "people first"?*

I think "people first" is everything. When we win a pitch, it's not only about our work and the product, it's also about the people. Our greatest clients are invariably the people we really get on with. New projects come from relationships. As much as people might write and talk about my design for a hotel, they're going back to it because of the person who greeted them at the concierge's desk, the person who was their bartender for the night. It doesn't matter how technologically driven the world gets, people will still matter. In my opinion, the more technologically enthralled we become, the more people will play an important role, especially within the hospitality industries. The human dimension of an experience has to matter, but as I'm saying this I'm imagining C-3PO mixing me a cocktail in a new bar, and he'd probably be fantastic. So everything I've said might mean nothing. But the most important thing is that we try, we really make an effort to come up with designs for places we think will be worthy of today and embraced by tomorrow.

# Hotel Russell

LATITUDE: 51.5, LONGITUDE: -0.1

LOCATION: RUSSELL SQUARE, LONDON, UK

CLIENT: STARWOOD CAPITAL GROUP / PRINCIPAL HOTELS

COMPLETING: 2017

Tara Bernerd & Partners was recently commissioned to design the refurbishment of the iconic Hotel Russell, in the historic heart of Bloomsbury, a stone's throw from the British Museum. Originally designed in 1898 by the fin-de-siècle architect Charles Fitzroy Doll, this landmark hotel is the hospitality sector's equivalent of a grand and stately home. It is notable not only for its impressive Renaissance-revival terracotta facade, which runs along one side of Russell Square, but also for its dining room that is said to be almost identical to the one Doll famously designed for the ill-fated RMS *Titanic*. Bernerd , together with partners Tommy Gymnander and Stephanie Weatherly, understood that working within the context of such a historic building called for deft handling, that if one was to return this Grade II listed building to its former glory, then the "new" had to be culturally sensitive to the "old." For instance in the lobby, with its extraordinary zodiac floor mosaic and towering marble pillars, Bernerd, Tommy Gymnander, and their team looked to humanize the space by adding a welcoming fireplace flanked by soft-edge sofas in complementary hues—thereby cleverly transforming this formerly echoing and somewhat imposing chamber into a welcoming human-scale space while retaining all its Victorian grandeur. Likewise, the wood paneling in the reception area gives a nod to the building's historic associations, yet still retains a contemporary quality—it is not copying the past, but rather channeling it.

This theme also runs through the design for the hotel's Palm Court, which was envisioned as the building's all-important social-lifestyle hub—a place for meeting, socializing, and relaxing. Because of planning constraints, Bernerd and the team were unable to completely open up the ceiling as they had initially hoped; however, their sympathetic approach reinstated some of the building's original ceiling design with subtle backlighting, which was used to create the illusion of a glass roof and lift the entire room with light. They also cleverly reconfigured the existing floor plan by introducing a walled fireplace and glass Crittall doors that lead onto a cocooned, open-air space perfect for intimate gatherings. The 370 bedrooms and suites were completely redesigned so that the interior layouts now meet the needs and considerations of today's modern guest while paying respect to the building's rich past. Even the corridors connecting the guestrooms have a contemporary-meets-antique aesthetic, with their tasseled bell-pulls outside each room and Victorian-style showerheads in the bathrooms functioning as evocative touches and tributes to the hotel's history. Describing herself as "a custodian," Bernerd and her team have employed elegant space planning and sensitive design to restore this iconic landmark to its former glory.

The Palm Court

# Apartment in Central Park South

LATITUDE: 40.7, LONGITUDE: -73.9

LOCATION: CENTRAL PARK SOUTH, NEW YORK CITY, NEW YORK, USA
CLIENT: PRIVATE
COMPLETING: 2016

right: Sculptures by Frederick Eversley (left) and
Keith McCarter (center)

Having previously designed a home for this private client in London, Bernerd was commissioned to work up a full renovation, including all interior architecture and a design scheme, for a magnificent 3,000-square-foot penthouse in New York City. With its concrete-paneled entrance, iron-framed Crittall doors, and discreet wooden ceiling, the apartment overlooking Central Park exhibits a strong trademark TB&P aesthetic. The gallery-style lobby provides an immediate sense of arrival and sets the tone for the space as a whole. As you make your way into this expansive open-plan space, you are struck by just how skillfully Bernerd, together with Tommy Gymnander and her team, is able to delineate different living zones using raised levels and a room-dividing fireplace-cum-bookcase, which has become something of a signature feature. An elevated seating area in front of the apartment's vast windows also ensures that the stunning city views are fully captured. The interior's palette of warm grays and tans gives the apartment a homey yet masculine feel; the hues are a nod to the apartment's location, an echo of those of the surrounding skyline. The warm and neutral tones also provide a suitable gallery-like backdrop for the client's collection of contemporary art, which he specially commissions from well-known artists.

right: Artwork by Matthew Cusick: *Course of Empire (Mixmaster 2)*, 2006. Courtesy of the artist and Pavel Zoubok

274

# Chiswick Gate

LATITUDE: 51.4, LONGITUDE: -0.26

LOCATION: BURLINGTON LANE, CHISWICK, LONDON, UK

CLIENT: BERKELEY GROUP

COMPLETING: 2017

The founder and chairman of Berkeley Group Holdings, Tony Pidgley has for more than a decade been one of Tara Bernerd's valued clients. In fact, he gave Bernerd one of her first commissions to design the much-acclaimed The Exchange, in Crouch End, in 2002. This interesting residential project saw the transformation of an old British Telecom exchange building into a block of stylishly modern loft-style apartments. Moreover, the synergy between Bernerd and Pidgley has led over the years to a number of highly successful, large-scale residential developments, from designing the interiors for Terry Farrell's deluxe Petersham Houses in Richmond (2003) to the forthcoming One Blackfriars tower by SimpsonHaugh and Partners with St. George.

One of the key projects that Bernerd and her team are working on for Pidgley's Berkeley Group is Chiswick Gate, a large-scale residential development in West London comprising townhouses alongside one-, two-, and three-bedroom apartments. Combining intelligent space planning with classic TB&P design panache, the resulting interiors have a warm contemporary feel thanks to the skillful use of layering, texture, and color. As the developer notes, Bernerd's "mix of rough and smooth textures—velvet, glass, wood and metal—creates a warm and welcoming tapestry." Certainly, the interiors designed by Bernerd and her team possess a relaxed classic-yet-contemporary atmosphere that exudes an effortless and tranquil sophistication. As Bernerd notes, "This project really is all about cutting-edge yet refined London living in that it mixes loft-like apartments with elegant family homes. And in many ways, this is a key project for Berkeley because it is taking what they do to a whole new level of design-led luxury."

# Four Seasons Fort Lauderdale

LATITUDE: 26.1, LONGITUDE: -80.1

LOCATION: NORTH FORT LAUDERDALE BEACH BOULEVARD, FORT LAUDERDALE, FL, USA
CLIENT: FOUR SEASONS / FORT CAPITAL
COMPLETING: 2018

The new Four Season Hotel & Private Residences in Fort Lauderdale is being built on a site that spans one full block along the pristine Floridian oceanfront. It is set to be a major landmark on this stretch of coastline, becoming the first large-scale hospitality development in this part of the Gold Coast for almost a decade. Occupying 1.8 acres, the main tower will have a three-story podium base upon which will be a further 25 stories of accommodations, each unit boasting panoramic ocean views. Working closely alongside Kobi Karp Architecture, the lead architects based in Florida, Tara Bernerd & Partners has been appointed to undertake the full interior architecture and design of the building's lobbies, bars, all-day dining facilities, and spa, as well as 148 hotel rooms and 50 condominium hotel rooms and private residences. Leading the project, in collaboration with partners Michelle Hughes and Nicola Watkins, Tara aims to marry an elegance of the past with a sophisticated and fresh contemporary style that embraces everything the Four Seasons stands for globally. As Bernerd notes, "We are building the first hotel of this kind in an area set to become Miami's Riviera." The scheme for such an iconic building therefore reflects a timeless quality, yet still retains a warmth that is so integral to Bernerd's work. Her signature aesthetic of texture and color will ensure an atmosphere that encourages guests to relax in the comfort of their own home away from home.

The café bar

# One Park Drive

LATITUDE: 51.4, LONGITUDE: -0.01

LOCATION: WOOD WHARF, ISLE OF DOGS, LONDON, UK

CLIENT: CANARY WHARF GROUP

COMPLETING: 2019

Exterior architectural design by Herzog & de Meuron

In the middle of a global city, space is always at a premium—so the more you can maximize the square footage of a building's internal area, the better. For this landmark 55-story tower in London's Docklands, designed by Herzog & de Meuron, that is exactly the role of Tara Bernerd & Partners as the designated interior architectural designer. Bernerd was appointed by Sir George Iacobescu of Canary Wharf Group, and she began work on the project by studying the floor plans with her team in minute detail so that they could best orient the tower's 452 apartments. The building has been divided into three zones, known as loft (base), cluster (middle), and bay (top), each with its own highly complex floor plate. The first thing that the team did was to work off a complex floor-layout grid for each zone, which included a mix of studio, one-bedroom, two-bedroom, and three-bedroom apartments on each floor. The next step was to focus on the layout of these variously sized apartments. As Bernerd recalls, "We spent nearly a year just working out the layouts." Following on from this stage was the creation of three levels of spec for the apartments.

However, rather than approaching this project from the standpoint of individual residential units, Bernerd and partners Michelle Hughes and Nicola Watkins took a more holistic view, recognizing that what they were really doing was designing and building lifestyles. This meant that the public areas and the private ones needed to be integrated as intelligently as possible. Likewise, careful consideration had to be given not only to making the apartments functionally efficient, but also to determining how that function might change over the course of a day. For instance, recognizing that people want their living rooms to be both comfortable places to live as well as sensational spaces for entertaining, Bernerd and her team's intelligent approach to space planning and design reflects the needs and wants of modern life. From initial layout designs to fixtures and finishes, careful consideration was paid to creating a depth and character true to the building, evoking a strong sense of place within one of the world's most iconic cities.

# Selected Projects

2001
Battersea Loft, London, UK; Private

2002
London Apartments, London, UK; Henry & James
White Cube Hoxton, London, UK; White Cube Gallery

2003
The Exchange, Crouch End, London, UK; Berkeley Homes
Petersham Houses, London, UK; Berkeley Homes
Grosvenor Dock, London, UK; St James
Riverside Lewes, East Sussex, UK; Rees Elliot

2004
The Old Bank, London, UK; Private Client
Sejour, London, UK; Sejour
Grange Road, East Sussex, UK; Rees Elliot

2005
82 Old Church Street, London, UK; Londonewcastle
Bromyard Avenue, London, UK; Berkeley Homes
The Grand Store, Royal Arsenal, London, UK; Berkeley Homes
The Knightsbridge, London, UK; The Knightsbridge

2006
Aspinalls, London, UK; Aspinalls Foundation
The Shooting Lodge, Devon, UK; Private Client
Paddington Penthouse, London, UK; Chelsfield Partners
St John's Square, London, UK; Londonewcastle

2007
Center Parcs Lodges, Nationwide, UK; Center Parcs/Blackstone
Wallpaper Factory, London, UK; Londonewcastle
64 Sloane Street, London, UK; Aspinalls Foundation
Marco Grill, London, UK; Chelsea Football Club/
    Marco Pierre White
Raffles, London, UK; Raffles Private Members Club
R20, London, UK; R20 Limited
The Armouries, Royal Arsenal, London, UK; Berkeley Homes

2008
67 Brook Street, London, UK; Chelsfield Partners
Chalet Miramonti, Gstaad, Switzerland; Private Client
Hive Bethnal Green, London, UK; J.G. Land
Hive Old Street, London, UK; J.G. Land
Aldford Street, London, UK; Private Client

2009
Swissotel Basel, Basel, Switzerland; Swissotel
Swissotel Zurich, Zurich, Switzerland; Swissotel
Aspinalls, London, UK; Aspinalls Foundation
Arundel Square, London, UK; Londonewcastle
MY *Cheeky Tiger*, Monte Carlo, Monaco; Private Client
West Range, Royal Arsenal, London, UK; Berkeley Homes
Villa Sa Torre, Mallorca, Spain; Private Client

2010
The Henson, London, UK; Londonewcastle
33B Westminster Terrace, Hong Kong; Grosvenor Asia/Asia Standard
Westminster Terrace Penthouse, Hong Kong; Grosvenor Asia/
    Asia Standard
Sunseeker Predator Yacht, Hong Kong; Private Client
HighCliff Penthouse, Hong Kong; HighCliff
Cassis, London, UK; Marlon Abela Restaurant Corporation
Mortons Club, London, UK; Marlon Abela Restaurant Corporation

2011
Strata Penthouse, London, UK; Brookfield Multiplex
Setai Apartment, Miami, USA; Private Client
Center Parcs Treehouses, Nationwide, UK; Center Parcs/Blackstone

2012
Belgraves, London, UK; Thompson Hotels/Harilela Group
Hix at Belgraves, London, UK; Mark Hix/Thompson Hotels/
    Harilela Group
Leman Street, London, UK; Berkeley Homes
Maida Vale Home, London, UK; Private Client

2013
Central Park West Apartment, New York, USA; Private Client
Riverside Apartment, London, UK; Private Client
MY *Orient Star*, Istanbul, Turkey; Private Client
Private Club at The Heron, London, UK; Heron International
Thompson Chicago, Chicago, USA; Thompson Hotels
Nico Osteria at Thompson Chicago, Chicago, USA;
   Thompson Hotels/One-Off Hospitality
Pont Street at Belgraves, London, UK; Thompson Hotels/
   Harilela Group

2014
SIXTY SoHo, New York; SIXTY Hotels
The Natural Kitchen, London, UK; The Natural Kitchen

2015
Port Lympne Treehouse Hotel, Kent, UK; Aspinall Foundation
Chelsea Creek Penthouses, London, UK; St George
Queens Gate, Shanghai, China; Couture Homes/Asia Standard

2016
Glasshouse Gardens, London, UK; Lend Lease
Kidbrooke Village, London, UK; Berkeley Homes
One the Elephant, London, UK; Lend Lease
Fulham Reach, London, UK; St George
Kensington Row Penthouses, London, UK; St Edward
Kau to Highland, Hong Kong; Couture Homes/Asia Standard
Central Park South Penthouse, New York, USA; Private Client

2017
Chiswick Gate, London, UK; Berkeley Homes
Hotel Russell, London, UK; Starwood Capital
The Hari Hotel Restaurant, London, UK; Harilela Group

2018
Four Seasons Fort Lauderdale, Fort Lauderdale, USA;
   Four Seasons/Fort Capital
Thompson Hollywood, Los Angeles, USA; Thompson Hotels
One Blackfriars, London, UK; St George
Perkins Road, Hong Kong; Couture Homes/Asia Standard

2019
One Park Drive, London, UK; Canary Wharf Group
K1, London, UK; Chelsfield Partners
The Hari, Hong Kong; Harilela Group

# Acknowledgments

MY THANKS AND DEDICATION TO:

My Partners: David Beck, Lucien Smith, Michelle Hughes,
Nicola Watkins, Stephanie Weatherly and Tommy Gymnander
Katherine Goodwin
All the team at Tara Bernerd & Partners

Charlotte and Peter Fiell
Mark Thomson
Charles Miers
Ian Luna, Meaghan McGovern and Monica Adame Davis
at Rizzoli

FOR THEIR SUPPORT OVER THE YEARS, THANKS TO:

Aron Harilela
The Archer Family
Camron PR
Chris Norton
Damian Aspinall
Dino Lalvani
Sir David Li
Elliott Bernerd
Sir George Iacobescu
Harland Miller
Harrison Le Frak
Hayley Sieff
Jay Jopling
John Hitchcox
John Pritzker
Kemper Hyers
Lubna Olayan
Michael Platt
Sir Mick Jagger
Nadim Ashi
Nick Loup
Philippe Starck
The Pomeranc Family
Richard Heyman
Richard and Ruthie Rogers
The Rug Company
Sue Crewe
Susan Bernerd
The Taskent Family
Thomas Griem
Tim Jefferies
Tony Pidgley
Victor Olivo

ARTWORK

Alan Wheatley Art
Ben Brown Fine Arts
Contemporary by Angela Li
Exhibition A
Hamiltons Gallery, London
Indiewalls Inc.
Little Black Gallery
White Cube

PHOTO CREDITS

Philip Vile: 12–13, 17, 19–37, 47–63, 85, 89, 90, 93, 95–101, 115,
117–125, 130–139, 141, 143–159, 167, 169–183, 185, 187–205, 207,
209–215, 218–225, 259, 261–263, 266–269
Adrian Gaut: 227, 229–243
Benedict Johnson: 8
Bill Batten: 83, 86–88, 91
Bob Carlos Clarke: 38
Center Parcs: 103, 105–113
Darren Chung: 45, 63
Edmon Leong: 126–129
Graciela Cattarossi: 4, 252
Heiner Orth: 65, 67–81
Jason Alden: 160
Luke Foreman: 245, 247–251
Maurizio Galimberti: 6
Randall Slavin: 10
Thompson Chicago: 216–217

CGIs:
Berkeley Homes: 277, 279
Canary Wharf Group & Visualisation One: 291, 293–299
Tara Bernerd & Partners: 264–265, 271, 273–275, 281, 283–289

First published in the United States of America
by Rizzoli International Publications, Inc.
300 Park Avenue South, New York, NY 10010
www.rizzoliusa.com

*Tara Bernerd: Place*
Design: © Tara Bernerd & Partners
Preface: © Tara Bernerd
Texts: © Tara Bernerd & Partners

*For Tara Bernerd & Partners:*
Managing Editors: Charlotte & Peter Fiell
Project Management: Katherine Goodwin

Designed by Mark Thomson

*For Rizzoli International Publications*
Editor: Ian Luna
Project Editors: Monica Adame Davis &
Meaghan McGovern
Production: Maria Pia Gramaglia &
Kaija Markoe
Design Coordination: Kayleigh Jankowski

Publisher: Charles Miers

Cover image: Photo by Philip Vile, featuring
artwork by Keith McCarter and Terry O'Neill

Printed in China

2017 2018 2019 2020 / 10 9 8 7 6 5 4 3 2 1
Library of Congress Control Number:
2016954146
ISBN: 978-0-8478-5861-3